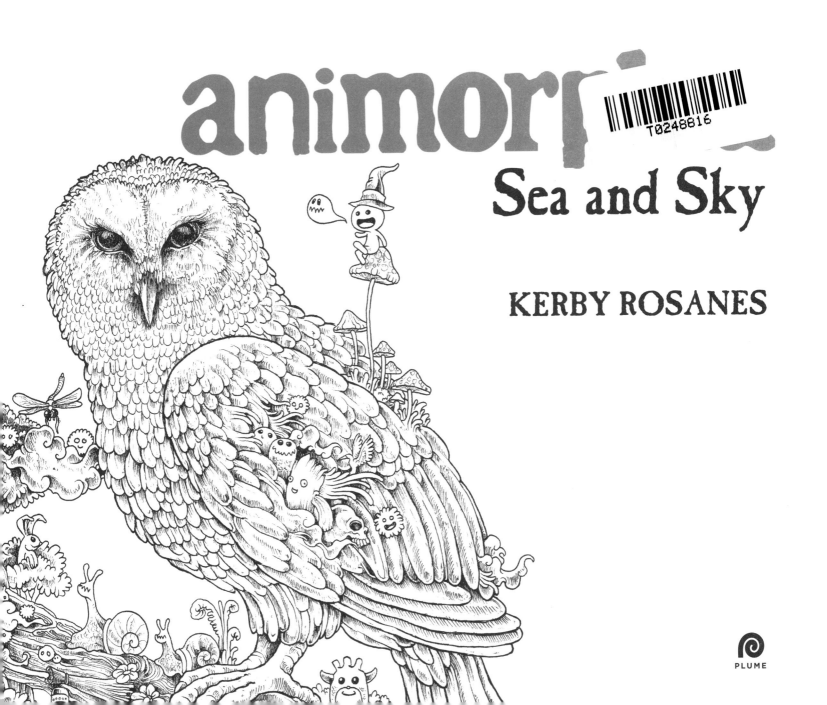

animorphia

Sea and Sky

KERBY ROSANES

PLUME

Illustrated by
Kerby Rosanes

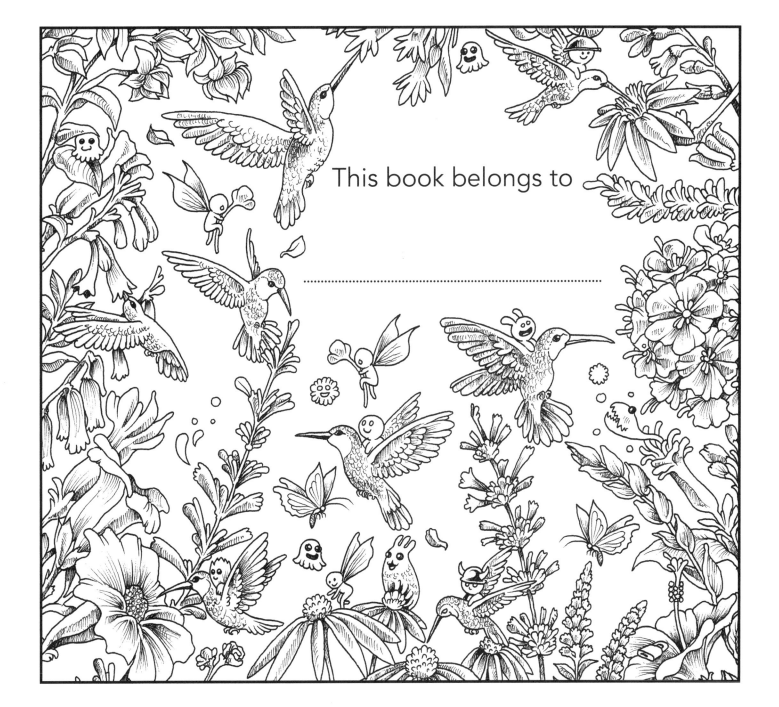

This book belongs to

....

Illustrated by Kerby Rosanes
Edited by Johnny Marx
Designed by Zoe Bradley

With thanks to Hannah Thornton
for being a great talent scout

PLUME
An imprint of Penguin Random House LLC
penguinrandomhouse.com

First published in Great Britain in 2015 by
LOM ART, an imprint of Michael O'Mara Books Limited,
9 Lion Yard, Tremadoc Road, London SW4 7NQ

mombooks.com
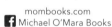 Michael O'Mara Books
 OMaraBooks
lomartbooks

ISBN 9780593188637

Printed in China
1 3 5 7 9 10 8 6 4 2

Create more creatures riding the waves.

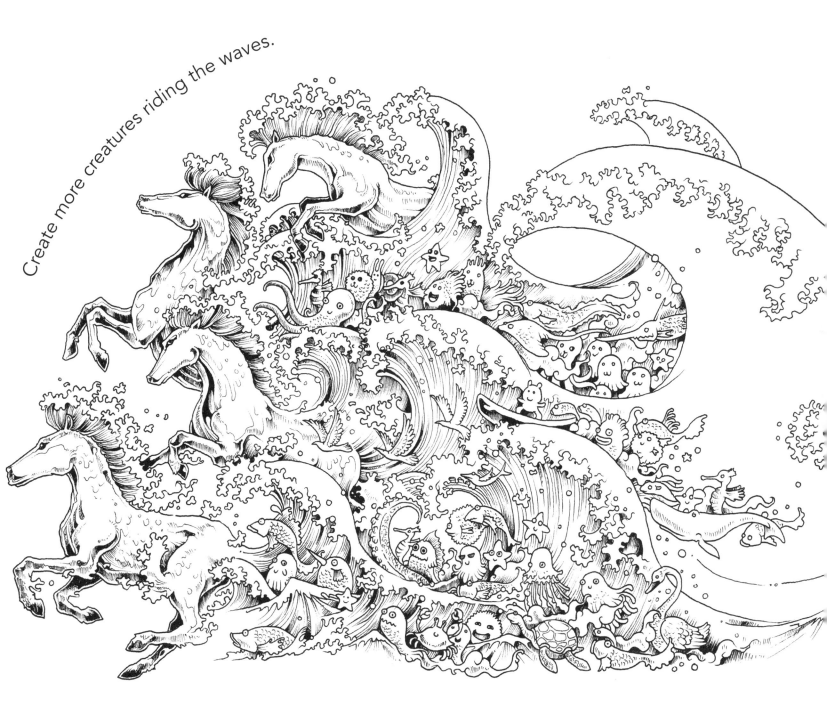

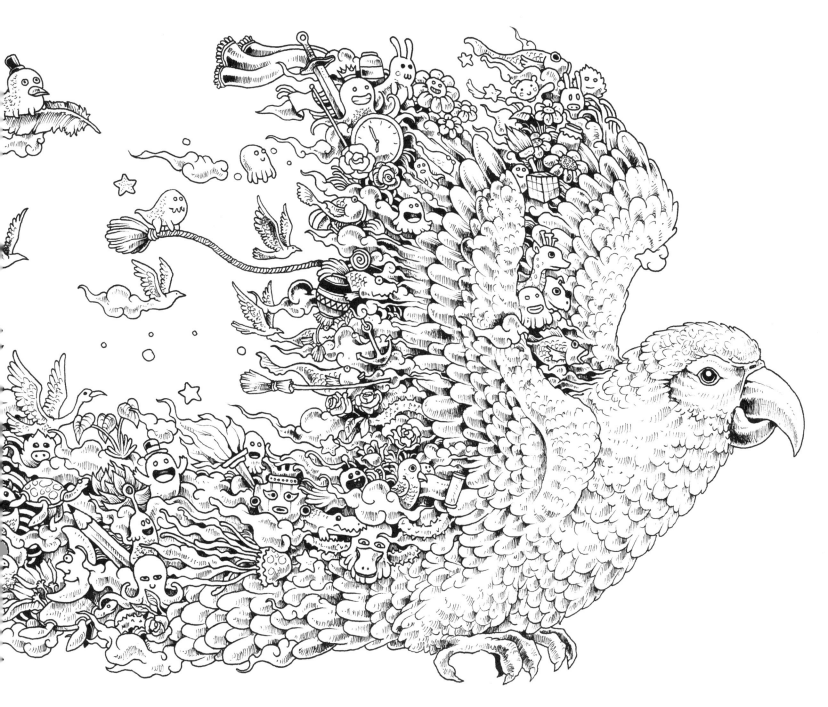

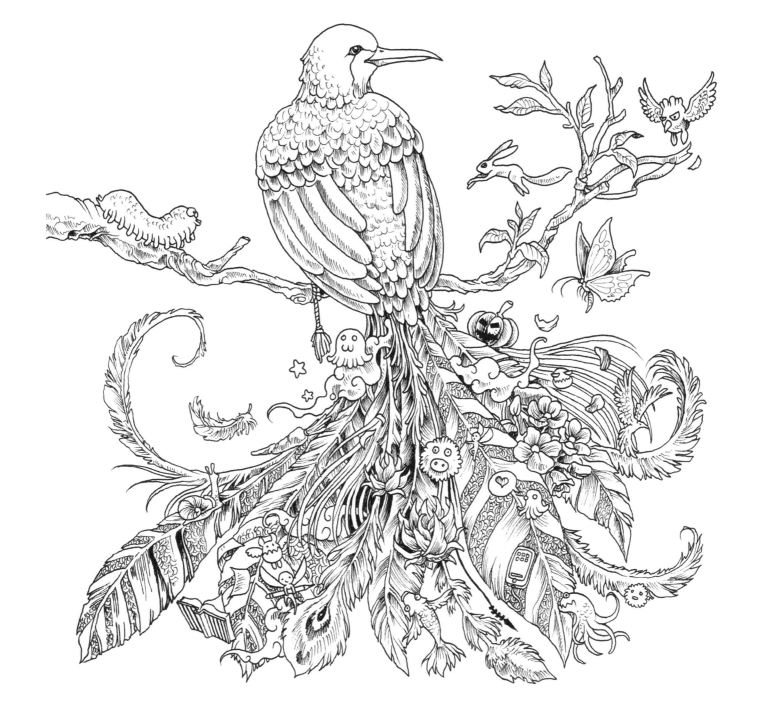

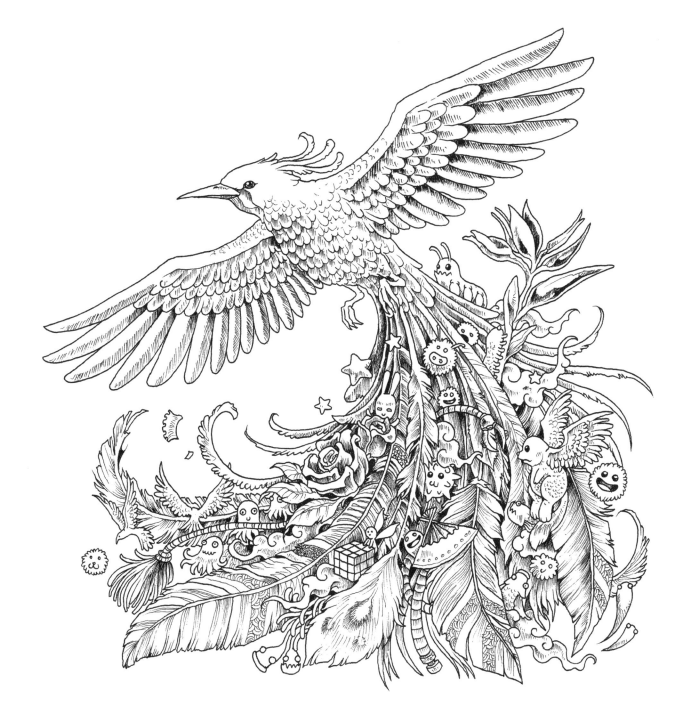

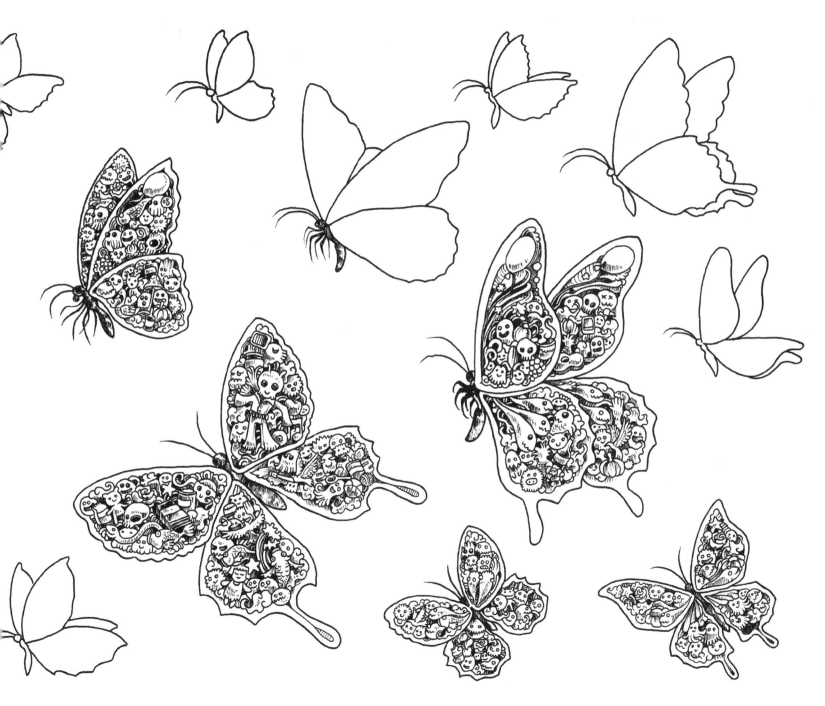

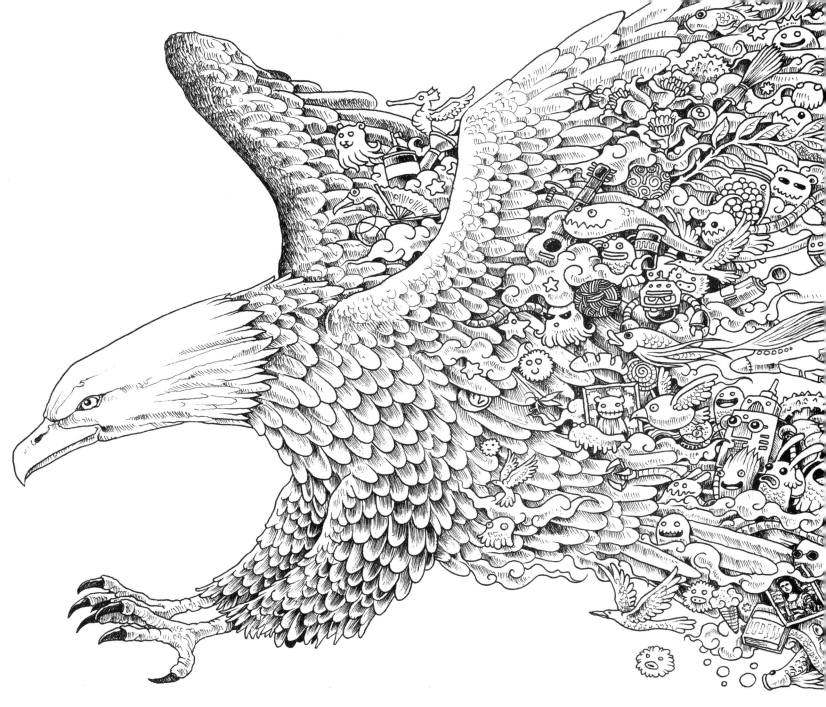

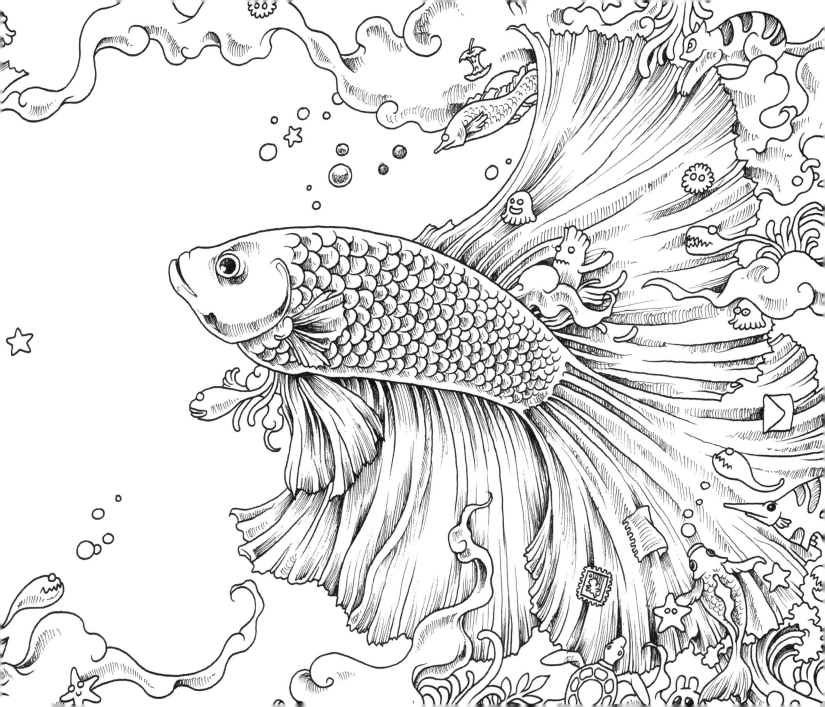

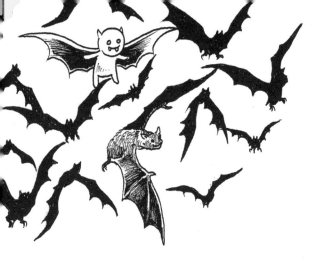

Fill the page with bats.

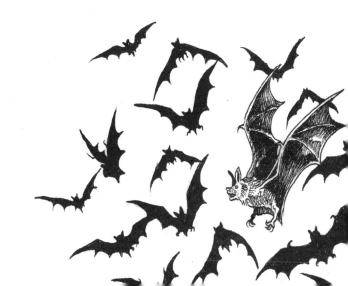

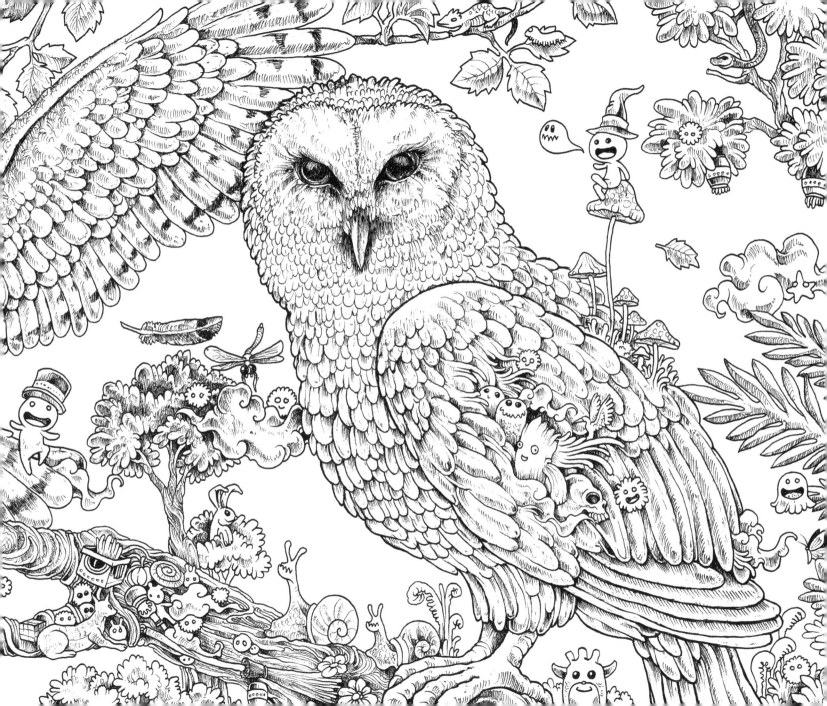

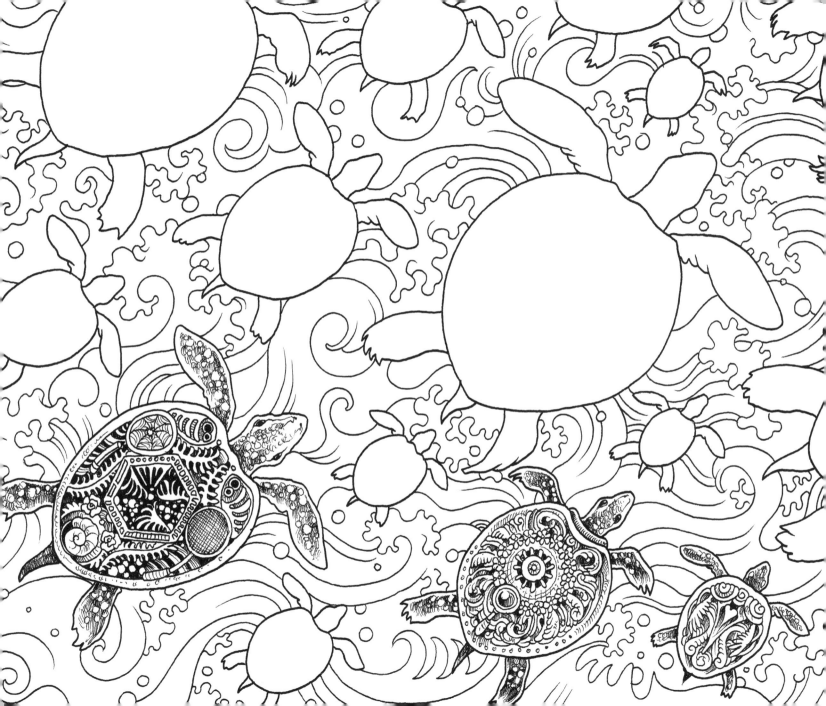

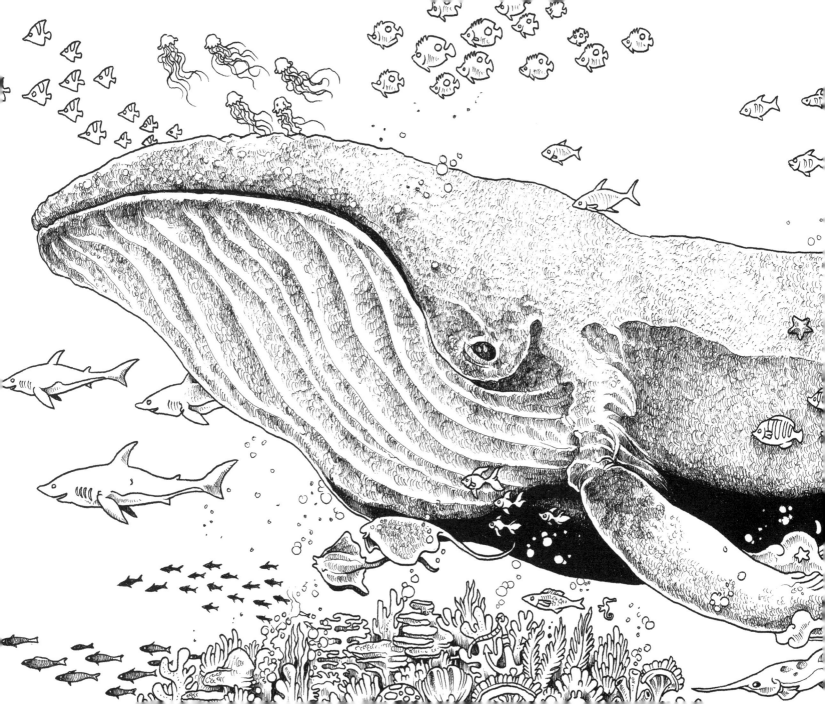

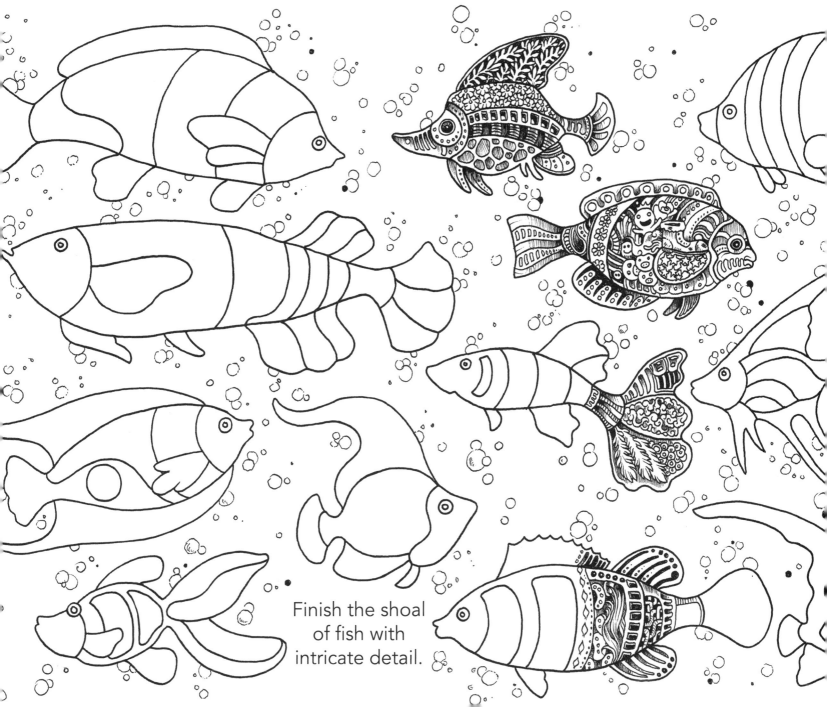

Finish the shoal
of fish with
intricate detail.

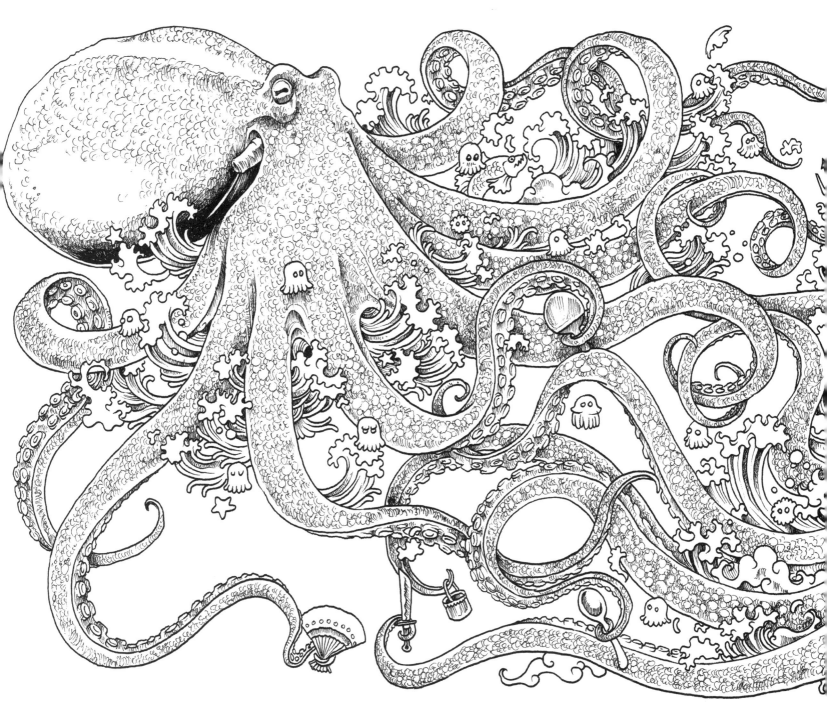

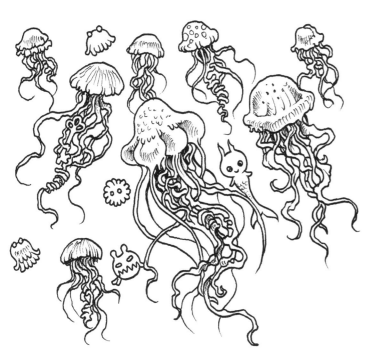

Draw more jellyfish to fill the page.

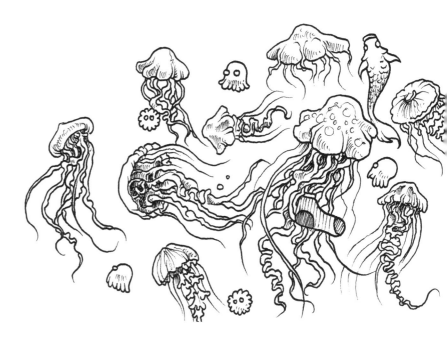

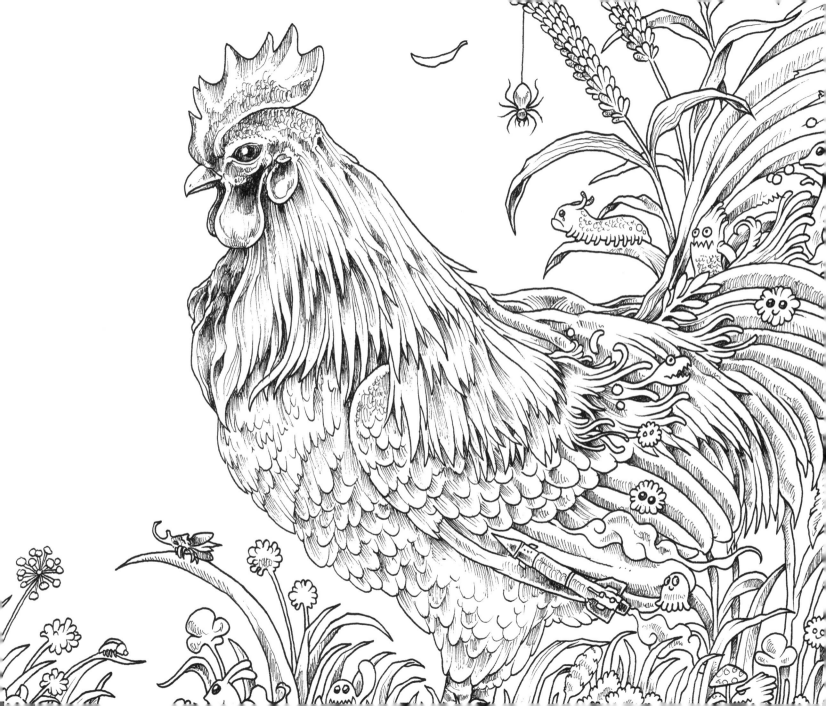

Complete this
pod of orcas.

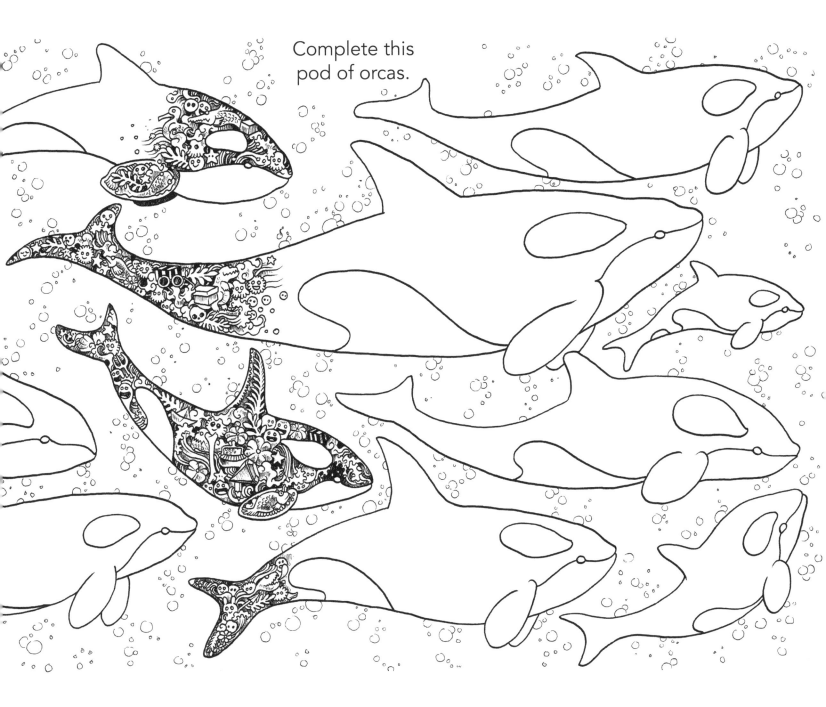

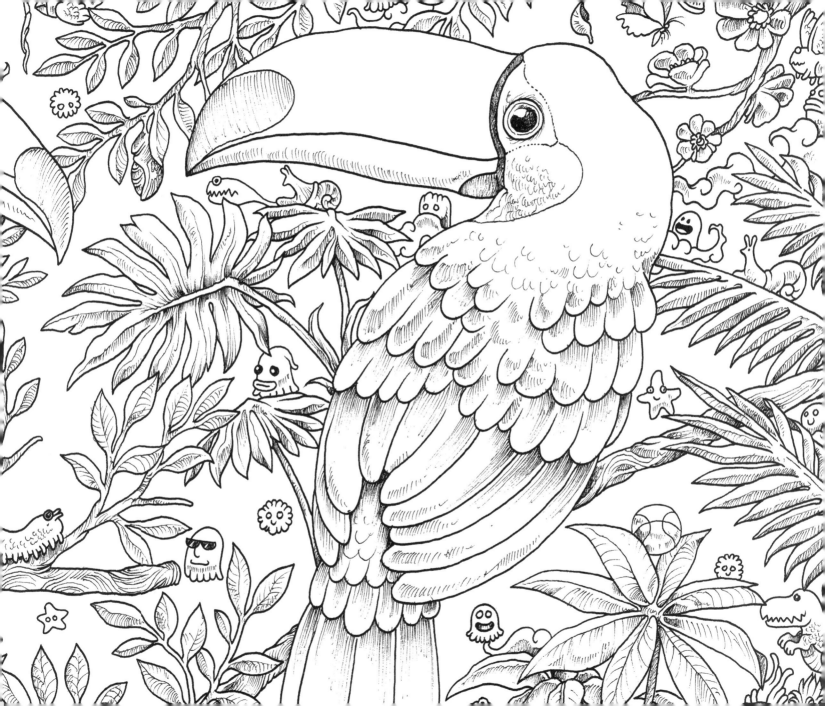

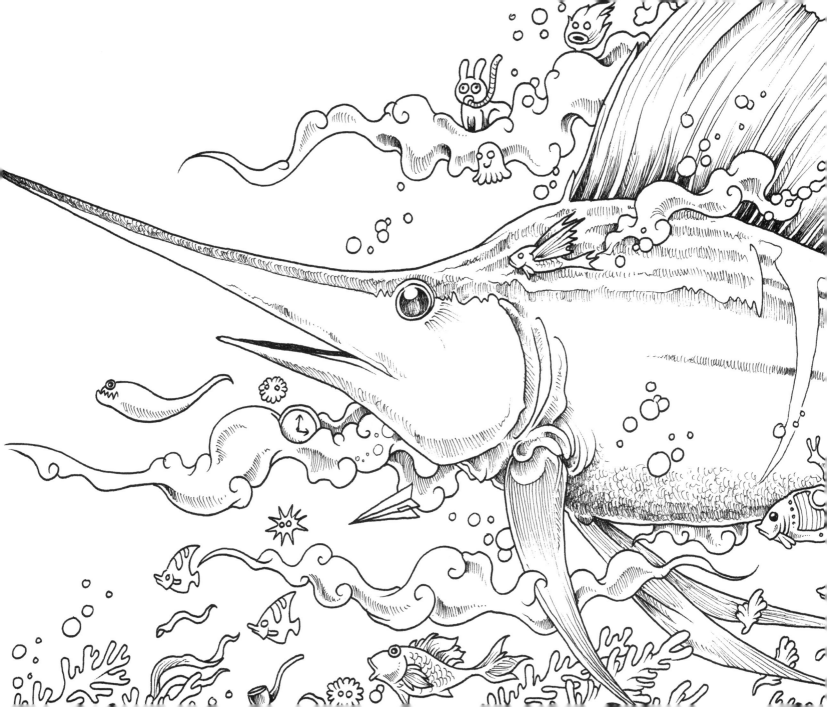

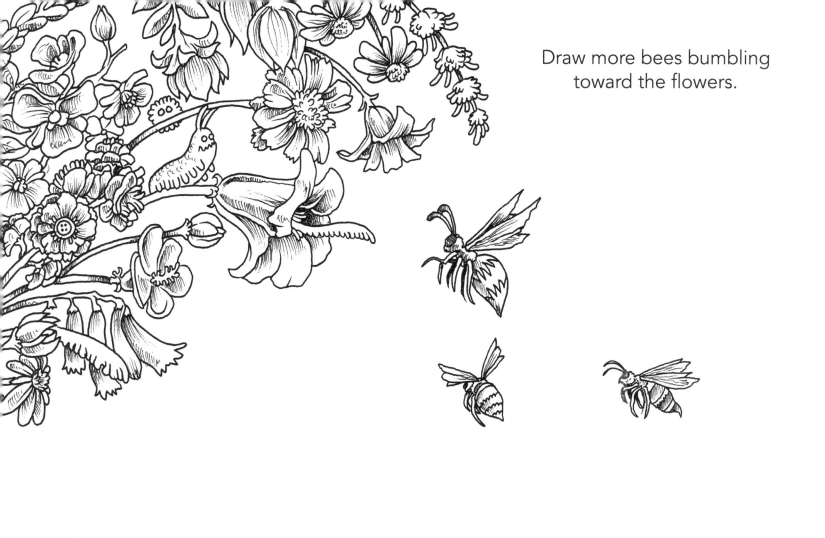

Draw more bees bumbling
toward the flowers.

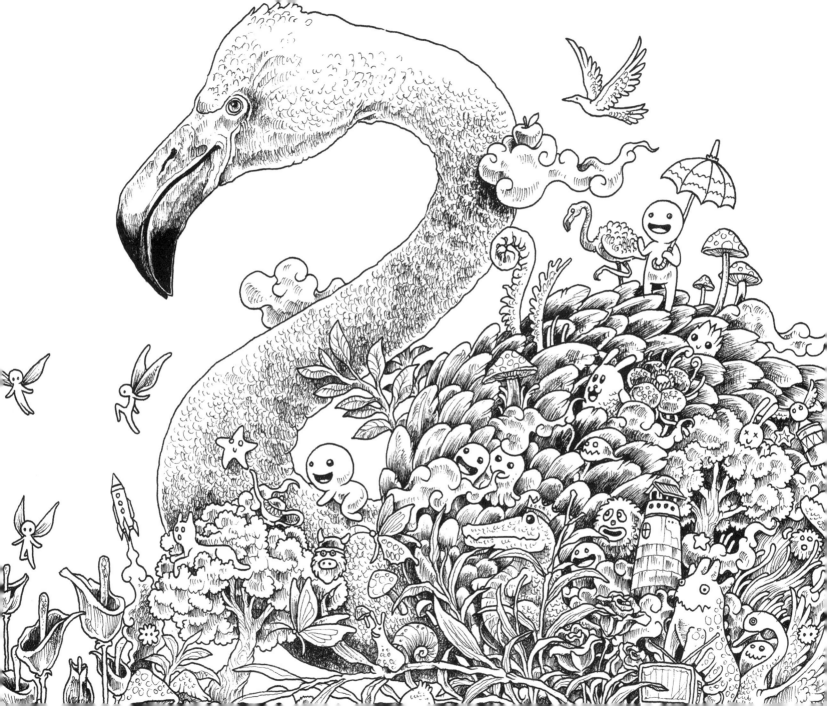

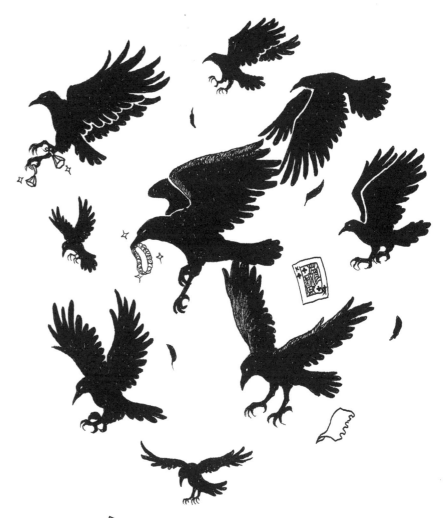

Doodle more crows.

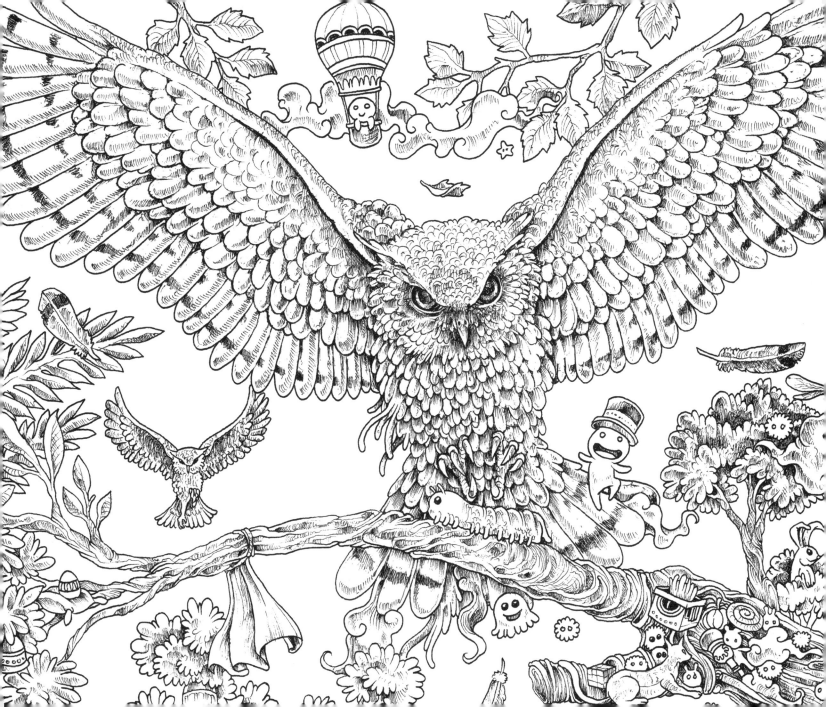